T0304456

Praise for Circle Tour

"In *Circle Tour* Eva Tihanyi not only poses the question, what does it mean to make art and meaning in an uncertain world?, she pulls us into this question and the act of questioning. 'The artist is more than present' in these poems, but—more than that—we are invited to be present too. A journey through the concentric circles of Tihanyi's carefully structured book is a coming-to-presence. *Circle Tour* is a powerful collection that challenges us to rethink the nature and potential of lyric poetry as a mode of human contact and imaginative response."

—**Johanna Skibsrud**, author of *The Description of the World*, *The Poetic Imperative: A Speculative Aesthetics*, and the Giller-Prize winning novel *The Sentimentalists*

"A lyrical, big-hearted celebration of what it takes to remain whole and hopeful, come what may."

—**Rona Maynard**, author of *My Mother's Daughter* and former Editor of *Chatelaine*

"Eva Tihanyi has done for stalwart love what Sylvia Plath did for despair. She examines it from every angle. She chronicles pain she has suffered in the past, and then does a stellar job of recounting how she left it behind. *Circle Tour* is erudite, uplifting, and completely honest."

—**Catherine Gildiner**, author of *Good Morning, Monster* and the three-volume memoir *Too Close to the Falls*, *After the Falls*, and *Coming Ashore*

"*Circle Tour* is exquisite. So many times I resisted turning a page, needing to remain with a single poem for a day. Two days. Three. However long it took for the lines to change the way I see."

—**Darcie Friesen Hossack**, Commonwealth Writers' Prize nominee and Managing Editor of *WordCity* Literary Journal

"Eva Tihanyi's wise, accomplished *Circle Tour* explores what it is to be human, under the stars, even in an imperfect world. Some poems acknowledge our troubled times, sorrow and loss, but ultimately turn toward hope and love, counselling us to go forward, not to look back. Tihanyi's pure poetry leads us through a section of her life journey and is a welcome companion on our own."

—**Elizabeth Greene**, author of *A Season Among Psychics* and *Understories*

"With language that is direct and philosophical, secular and sacred, Eva Tihanyi guides us on a *Circle Tour* that is a quest for quietude in a turbulent world. Along the way, she contemplates nature, politics, art and family as she spirals toward a meditation upon 'the soul's topology,' its 'potent brimming.' Here, where the 'wind has no volition, / the stone no voice,' this eloquent poet retains 'a calloused trust in the goodness of things.'"

—**Karen Shenfeld**, author of *To Measure the World*

Circle Tour

Also by Eva Tihanyi

Fiction

Truth and Other Fictions

Poetry

The Largeness of Rescue
Flying Underwater: Poems New and Selected
In the Key of Red
Wresting the Grace of the World
Restoring the Wickedness
Saved by the Telling
Prophecies Near the Speed of Light
A Sequence of the Blood

Circle Tour

POEMS

Eva Tihanyi

Toronto, Ontario, Canada
www.inanna.ca

The publisher gratefully acknowledges the support of the Canada Council for the Arts and the Ontario Arts Council. The publisher is also grateful for the financial assistance received from the Government of Canada.

Cover design: Val Fullard

Library and Archives Canada Cataloguing in Publication

Title: Circle tour / poems by Eva Tihanyi.
Names: Tihanyi, Eva, author.
Series: Inanna poetry & fiction series.
Description: Series statement: Inanna poetry & fiction
Identifiers: Canadiana (print) 20220456194 | Canadiana (ebook) 20220456267 | ISBN 9781771338936 (softcover) | ISBN 9781771338943 (EPUB) | ISBN 9781771338950 (PDF)
Subjects: LCGFT: Poetry.
Classification: LCC PS8589.I53 C57 2023 | DDC C811/.54—dc23

Printed and bound in Canada

Inanna Publications and Education Inc.
210 Founders College, York University
4700 Keele Street, Toronto, Ontario M3J 1P3 Canada
Telephone: (416) 736-5356   Fax: (416) 736-5765
Email: inanna.publications@inanna.ca Website: www.inanna.ca

For Jeanne—
full circle

Contents

Outer Circle

Inner Circle

Centre

We came whirling out of nothingness,
scattering stars like dust...
The stars made a circle, and in the middle,
we dance.

—Rumi

I've been circling for thousands of years
and I still don't know: am I a falcon,
a storm, or a great song?

—Rainer Maria Rilke

Outer Circle

Hope

If you're reading this,
you're still here.

The Eye Is the First Circle

In time we confront
the circle of our story—
or is it a spiral really?

Upward or downward,
depending.

It matters, how we see it.

When you're caught in a circle,
a leap is the only way out.

The Given

In the beginning there's always a road
but all roads end, and time owes us nothing.

Memory orders up the old defeats,
dredges the past forgotten days.

The heart waxes and wanes
predictable as the moon.

The obliging sun does not distinguish
between good and evil.

The wind has no volition,
the stone no voice.

Our pixilated souls consider nothing,
can't see their million mirror shards.

This is how we travel
(sometimes aware, sometimes not)
to the inevitable.

Eclipse

The world turns its eyes
to the heavens.

The moon blocks the sun,
another media event:
celestial celebrity.

The world looks for metaphor
while the moon orbits
the earth and the earth
orbits the sun
which couldn't care less,
continues burning.

Your face hidden from me
(for a moment)
by your hand.

The bright ring of light
frames an utter darkness—
harbinger.

A Hellish Season

The discovery of innocence is its loss
yet amidst the sanctioned ugliness,
to take the risk of beauty—
that's the rise of living!

Some call this a mottled faith,
an ersatz version of impending zero,
but it's not nothing.

Across the uncivilized terrain
where predators binge and walls are terminal:
so many exits into the afterlife,
souls rife with arriving.

It's here that we bed down
with the miracle worker, dream
of the vanishing point, try to gain
our agency even as it negates us.

The only questions left:
What did you try to save?
What wreckage did you win?

History

Amid the sad changes
the depths discover us
and the dormant losses
reappear, new questions
acknowledging history.

This is the way of knowing, this
the dark at the sun's heart.

Sooner or later tragedy
will trump distance, arrive
at your doorstep.

Believe me:
what you wish for
will make not
the slightest difference.

Encounter

1.

Here you are.
I've been waiting.

Will you let me
share the wind's call, the life-force
of keen greening, the all-seeing sun
as it summers down
on the needy world?

Will you stay by my side
as all the things we've lost
fall upon us, their weight gaining
in the treacherous hours of night?

Will you enter into
the no-turning-back of love,
eyes open, your will free,
your hands reaching?

What will be your stance
in our unchosen world?

The sky stirs,
the shadows stretch.

There is time in everything.

2.

The words hide
but we must find them.

It's an earnest business,
manufacturing truth, the grand edifice
of power.

Everything comes, leaves,
season by season.

Have you noticed?

There are those
who revel in their vile chaos,
and whatever was for years
slouching toward us
is now irrevocably born.

It hurts, this darkness.

Did I tell you?
The fear welled up in me
and I cried.

But then the carapace of longing broke,
and I subsided.

Resistance

Sometimes you feel your brokenness,
the futility of betterment.

Your heart has run out of promises
like a vehicle out of fuel.

This is when age overtakes you,
both yours and the world's.

The day when despair falls like heavy rain
and you have no coat.

Why resist, your empty heart says.
Why resist anything?

Do You Know

The world is more fucked up than it's ever been.

Do you know the oceans are drowning in themselves,
the sun is eating itself alive?

That deaths are coming faster than you can count,
and every day there's a new lie about solutions?

Do you know you'll be outlived
by glass and metal, Styrofoam and plastic?

That the conjunction of planets
and the alignment of stars don't matter?

Do you know that unequivocal Power
considers itself holy?

That fate decreed you favoured,
gave you choices, conferred your worth?

Do you know that if you wreck yourself
on the rocks of language, you'll continue bleeding?

Celebration

January 20, 2021

We're grateful for all that we undid,
are astonished by our success.

There's nothing better
than a grand amazement.

And now there he is, the harbinger.

His face fistic with the rage of a deposed king,
he waddles past the tough crowd
into a future that will show no mercy.

Relieved, we watch the depraved one go,
forget for a moment
that he's not the first one
or the last one
or the only one.

The New Normal

We used to wish for adventure nights,
wild urban neon, rebel tales told
in vodka language, beer songs spilling
from summer windows.

Now we long for safe country sleep.

But still.

There is simmering
and fierce desire.

I'm in slow boil,
my heart a rogue's apothecary
of forbidden medicine.

Just wait, the hopeful voice says.
Wait for it.

Would It Be Enough

Would it be enough if you
had the courage to announce yourself, even if only in solitude?

Would it be enough if you
ceased looking for a plan in your palm (or anywhere)?

Would it be enough if you
stopped leaning into the future as if it were an adversary wind?

Would it be enough if you
allowed chance to teach you flight and freedom?

Would it be enough if you
let what's good make more of you?

Would it be enough if you
realized that each night you re-inherit the stars?

Don't Look Back

We remember, need to know,
crave the illusion of certainty,
but memory can't retrieve us.

Like Lot's wife we turn around
and are lost.

Think too of Orpheus
as he walks forward
and Eurydice follows.

He doesn't trust, looks back,
and so loses her forever.

Next, ahead, tomorrow:
hard to believe in the future
but we must.

Spring Meditation

Like the code of flowers
embedded in seeds
we carry our hope within us,
essential force.

I watch the robin perch
on my neighbour's willow,
marvel at the bird
living its birdness.

The large solace in small things:
the wave of a hand,
the single grass blade
in the field's vastness,
the lone branch,
the one leaf,
the sum total
of all our distances.

Defiance 1

There is nothing stable in the world; uproar's your only music.

—John Keats

There, among the hypnotic havoc
of galaxies that dream themselves into your dreams,
dance to the chaos, thrive in the madness,
embrace the unpredictable days.

Shirk abstinence,
shrug off the rain.

Seize the multi-hearted love,
the mutinous song.

Hold the furious fullness
which is utterly secular and utterly sacred.

You are inextricable
from this wild quickening.

Don't be well behaved.

Defiance 2

Through the exhortations of opening,
the passionate arrivals, despite
the frequent falterings,
continue the unfashionable
hunt for yourself.

Traverse the soul's topology, bear witness
to its concentric story.

Renounce the plots where even
the weeds are well organized.

Be your own epiphany.

Blaze bright, cast a shadow.

Eschatology

Our final appraisal won't tell much.

Like an unfinished sentence
meaning-bound but not arriving,
we console ourselves with nouns, remind each other
that history repeats and only the names change.

We forget: it's verbs that grant direction.

We ignore our victories, parse our sorrows,
watch with nervous eyes the spectacle
of push against constraint.

On the pages of now: the past,
indelibly present, a haunting watermark.

There's no avoiding the life-rush.

Before you know it, your small significance
will race like a spark through dry grass, with luck
burn wildly radiant before its rain-defeated ending.

In the meantime: release the words,
create your life the way music shapes time.

Bocelli Sings "Amazing Grace"

When he stands
alone
in front of Milan's Duomo
in his tuxedo
and sad bow tie,
the streets around him
empty, the whole city
locked away, the entire world
confined, waiting,
I bow my head to a faith
greater than all cathedrals.

Here

In the forest where music happens
with or without you, where
neither your presence nor consent
is necessary; where
amidst the prayer of leaves
and hymn of branches the gods
become worship worthy; where
all the histories of the heart
adhere, the border
where fear cedes to trust
and new hopes are seeded; here
in the bird realm, you will hear
the truest singing.

About Birds, Again

Above the lake
the Canada geese are forming, honk
their flight into the blue air
while the cardinal, feeder-perched,
calls out a tune
before its graceful bright trajectory.

Chickadee, sparrow, carping gull.
Jay, mourning dove, insistent woodpecker.
Robin, starling, red-winged blackbird.

Announcements of life returning:
the cooing and cawing,
warbling and chippering.

Listen to the birds,
their necessary songs.

Through them
the oldest worlds call out.

2020 Vision

The lake sings its blues
in this odd despondent summer like no other
when we sit apart cherishing the air.

Your heart beats, your lungs breathe,
your sad soul has been tempered
by sad knowledge, yet still it holds
a calloused trust in the goodness of things.

Don't hesitate: address the birds,
the trees, the flowers.

Tell the remarkable world how much,
despite itself, you love it.

Summer Reprieve

We head out to the field,
return with the day
still on our shoulders,
bring with us
the small sunlit branches
with which we'll fire the night,
ignore the irrefutable line
between life and death,
breath and silence.

And when next we wake
it will be again to the wheat
rising up, a golden revolution
marching for acres, the road
stretching, stretching.

Sunday Drive, Niagara

This, the landscape
of our "wild and precious" days.

The whisky light of late afternoon,
mellow and burnished, the Norway maples
ochre in the autumn sun.

Plume grass and fountain grass, chrysanthemums
yellow, burgundy, bronze.

The sumac, its red leaves like strong feathers.

Amber cornfields, grape clusters
dark with ripening.

In every direction, straights and turns
and new ways in.

When we love with attention,
all roads belong to us.

There Are Those Who Say

Why write about beauty
when all the world is stained
with grief and madness?

Why speak of suns and moons,
irrelevant stars?

Why sing of birds?

Why honour the trite trees
and their repeating leaf cycles?

Why pay tribute to the rain?

How will recording the ocean's moods
end injustice, poverty, the horrors of war?

How will your privileged poems
save the children?

What good can come
from your reckless word love,
your celebratory pages?

Ask yourself this.

Empathy

Like the fish
you know the shock
of the hook, the struggle
to break free, the jolt
of being jerked from home.

Know also the grace
of return, the hand
that releases, the rush
of welcome water.

You're not so different
from everything alive.

Two Views

From the Boat

The great wave rears up, primal
wrath of water, certain death.

You're no match for this,
a sudden novice
astonished and unnecessary.

Rapture: how you focus
on the distant mountain,
its white-capped solidity.

It's only in the end
that you discover
what you love.

Reprieve

Fine wind, clear morning.

The red mountain fills you
with survival, its potent brimming.

In this godly moment—eternal
time—you stand oddly silent
as if you belonged,
could truly see.

Experienced Music

I can't talk about my singing. I'm inside of it.
—Janis Joplin

1.

It didn't work for you—the crowd love—
in the end.

Not possible
to reconcile singular and plural,
the I and all the others (and in that truce
to find the no-rage of understanding).

It was your time, and not your time.
Your gift: to make of art an urgency.

Decades later, still it drives
a stake into the heart—your voice—
cleaves it open.

What you had in the end: the certainty
of aloneness, no comfort
in the stark aftermath of adulation.

It prevails: something alive
caught in your throat, howling.

2.

You didn't trust romance, craved it just the same,
your marrow a woman's marrow sweet and raw with longing,
your eye a woman's eye reckless and burning through.

Within the years of need, grief also.

You contain, but refuse to be contained.
The curse of hindsight: regret.
As you always said, you get what you settle for.

3.

Euphoria: when the tribe dances at your feet,
goddess of the profane and the deep wild.

Note by note you live what they can't.
You bay at the world as if it were the moon.

In the rude rebellious night, poised
on the edge of your darkest dreaming,
you are safe in your singing, holy animal.

4.

What is there to say?

That there is no end to anything
but eventually the endings.

That we surmise and negotiate
and give in to surrender.

That the music offers a brief respite
(glorious)
from the tyranny of waiting.

The day breaks already broken
yet still we hope.

Don't feel sorry.

Eat, and be comforted.
Drink, and be comforted.
The void is hungrier and thirstier
than you can imagine.
It cannot be consumed
by you, or anyone.

Strange day, when you realize
there is nothing but strangeness.

Erasures

1.

Erased de Kooning Drawing,
Robert Rauschenberg, 1953.

It happens like this:
Rauschenberg asks de Kooning
for one of his pencil drawings
so he can erase it—literally.

Some might see this
as an act of symbolic obliteration,
but the older artist (unthreatened)
agrees to the request.

He gives Rauschenberg a dense drawing
thick with crayon, charcoal, pencil—
something not easy to eliminate.

Rauschenberg is diligent,
erases for two months until
only the faintest outlines remain.

He hangs the piece in a gilded frame,
calls it a celebration.

2.

The Rhine II,
Andreas Gursky, 1999.

He photographs the Rhine near Düsseldorf
at the only straight stretch of the river.

There are realities in this picture:
several dog walkers, a factory smokestack, a ship,
trees on the horizon line.

Gursky wants perfect bands of colour,
visual purity, a return to original facts,
the river in its Eden state.

He manipulates the image, erases
what doesn't suit him: true view.

3.

The Face of the Lover,
------------, 2007.

A woman admires
her ex-lover's portrait of her.

She likes the way
she's been presented, wants to keep
this flattering version of herself present.

But the artist needs to be omitted
so she carefully erases the signature.

Now it's as if the portrait
had created itself.

Artist gone, subject intact.

A perfect vanity.

Regina

For Rose-Aimée Bélanger

You call them your *rounds*, smooth women
cast in fleshy bronze, various sizes,
the one on my desk your smallest.

She sits, little thinker,
insouciant queen, confident
as an egg, her dainty feet
pressed together, plump arms
around her knees, hugging herself.

I imagine she holds
birth in her, other mysteries.

Her hair is a mess of
short curls, her mouth open
slightly, on the verge
of speaking.

I am here, she will say.
Like it or not, it doesn't matter.

Marina Abramović at the Museum of Modern Art

Across the table
she faces the faces, one
by one, one
after the other.

Her long red dress
the robe of a priestess, worshipper
of silence, the artful gaze.

The artist is more than present.

She looks deeply, sees down,
pores to the very bottom.

She understands
that if you look long enough,
you will find the sky.

In my dream:
my eyes in hers, open;
my heart as full as the space
between two words,
and as empty.

Unexpected grace.

Imagine if all the stars fell
suddenly at your feet,
and you stepped into them
fearless and illuminated.

Cobalt Blue

Considering the art of Lisa Brice

Blue women in a louche world,
night denizens among the smoke and mirrors.

Theirs a profound nakedness,
the spirit undressed, both
self-contained and confrontational.

The irrational heart hidden within
the confines of pose and attitude,
an intimate indifference.

A fierce female answer
to the age-old gaze:
Look at us.
We owe you nothing.

A 21st Century Poem for Gloria Steinem

1.

Start with this: a man
on a sidewalk, a large man
on a narrow sidewalk, the sidewalk
in a midnight city, any season.

Across the street
a woman reaches her doorstep,
fumbles for keys in the darkness.

This could be 1972 or fifty years later.

Fear is timeless.

2.

No solace in windows
if there are no doors.

But when a woman understands herself,
she can bring down a world.

There is hope in this, always.

3.

I see my young self more clearly now
as one can see the whole forest
only from a distance.

She stands still as a tree,
her roots deepening.

Soon she will pull free, begin
her race toward comprehension.

Look at her run,
the fierce push in her.

She is intent on alighting.

Despite Everything

For Gloria Steinem

Despite everything we keep going
backward, believe always that
we're further ahead than we are.

We forget that if the sun hits it just right,
even the robin casts a shadow.

The story exceeds us, embitters
and enslaves, ennobles and enables,
and the darkness knows no borders.

Hope is a form of planning, you say.
Don't agonize. Organize.

Despite everything
we'll keep going.

Inner Circle

My Grandmother Continues

Not a day passes
that I don't think of you.

Your love the selvage
that averted my unravelling.

Your promise:
If you keep your eyes open,
you will be revealed.

A denizen of books,
an acolyte of the sun:
you were more than the sum
of your conjurings.

Because of you
I know that curating words
is not enough,
is more than enough.

Because of you
I dare to imagine Icarus
as a young girl, her heart
stuffed with feathers,
dreaming of flight.

Because of you
I dare to imagine her
not falling.

December

In memory of Luciana Ricciutelli

1.

Near the burnt-out end
of a precarious year,
you left us.

In the wake of your departure,
a terrible knowing: gone
means gone.

Yet a cadence continues, your voice
clear within us:
Dear hearts, keep writing.

2.

At the imagined borders
of ourselves, where death is,
we go beyond.

Not for you, a solemn jurisdiction.

Wherever you are,
there will be dancing.

3.

We remember you,
refute winter, argue
with the wind, refuse
to confirm the cold.

We remain rooted
in words, stand
firmly grounded.

We trust
in eventual spring, hope
that even the gravest silence
has a hole in it,
and the birds will sing through.

Courage

My poetry wanted them
and so they came, the tumultuous hours,
the bouts of love, the obsessions
like a fever.

Throughout it all, there you were,
friend of a lifetime, watching me
wend my way to adulthood,
my complex relationship with doors.

But the capricious moods of time,
inevitable, insistent as waves on rock,
wash over us, wear us down.

And the selves we were, less visible
with each passing year, recede
and diminish.

You knew me then,
you know me now.

To the end this will sustain me.

Come, let us link arms,
whistle bravely
into the gaining dark.

Another Harvest Moon

(For D.H. on her 65th)

Once again I think of you
on this annual autumn night,
your stalwart heart still tuned to spring,
your friendship a safety, always
an embrace.

So many vines have withered,
so many apples fallen.

Yet they return, as we do,
as the moon does also.

Let's raise our glasses then, toast
the cycles, celebrate the season,
sing together in the darkness
of nothing but the light.

Poem for My Brother

At 88 our obstinate father, determined
to die in his birth country,
moves back across the Atlantic.

Now, both abandoned
and released by his silence,
we are beyond his command
at last.

No need to list what we know so well,
the cruelties and injustices, the arrogant will:
father knows best, father is right,
father rules.

What we need are words of freedom,
not retribution—and so
I offer you new names for old hurts,
small ways of understanding
large events.

When we tried for a turn,
we failed, and the lines
never converged, they just
kept on running.

And yet: the times changed
and we changed with them.

Our youth we left behind long ago.

What he could not destroy between us:
the light of forever connection,
bright ampersand.

My Mother Nears Ninety

Her life took its time
diminishing; like Rome
it wasn't ruined in a day.

More and more still
in her stillness, she has become
a perfect secret, unknowable.

Her way of surviving
that inscrutable puzzle, the world.

If only she dared to make
a move, take that first step
forward from the past,
she might yet find at the road's end
a whole universe open-armed,
waiting.

In This Uneasy Spring

In this uneasy spring
my mother lies in a hospital bed,
dying.

Still she watches the war news,
others dying also.

The world in my mother,
my mother in the world.

One by one the walls fall,
all ruin revealed.

When finally her face
settles into peace, I see myself,
estranged bystander.

So little have I given her.

And in the end, there's only the end—
and compassion, which too is love.

My Mother Annotates a Book of My Poetry

1.

After her death
her penciled underlining
speaks like a code.

It begins with a scene:
he comes at her, shoves her
against a wall, and then
she's down, whimpering
Don't hurt me, don't hurt me.

What happens next:
she's embarrassed by herself, the way
she continues sitting with him
at the same table in the same house,
shoulders slumping.

Nine cans of beer between ten and four,
a woman's place no longer in the home
because she isn't safe in it.

They're partners in a private labyrinth,
one heartbroken, the other
enjoying the mood.

2.

What she remembers:

I was young once
and far more beautiful, and men
came knocking at my door—men
I didn't think were good enough,
but nothing's perfect, not even
thoughts in the head, certainly not
my myriad subversive synapses,
such aberrations.

I stare for hours at air, photo albums,
my whole body nothing but weight, mass,
the solidity that keeps me here.

Preferable not to think at all.

I chomp, I fawn, I am a sepulchre,
even at the apex a mere ventriloquism.

Through no fault of my own,
I am not who I am.

Cracked like a mosaic
left too long in the fire,
I dream of cold, of snow.

The days pass on, wash
over me in steady currents
as I lie motionless
in a fabulous absence of pain.

It's easy, this immersion,
like drowning.

I can say:
there was a birth,
the pain over, just beginning,
a love beyond love,
my child's name, a small melody.

I can say:
eventually she grew up.

What I can't say:
no matter what happens,
will she remember me.

Conversations with My Son

1.

I carry your history within me,
the things only I can remember,
the versions of you that only I know.

Everyone else has died
or was never there.

2.

It's not easy to be the parent or the child,
to admit the hard words or to listen.

I say: *I want you to know me*
but there's no such thing
as a perfect knowing.

And so we settle for less,
a compromise of understanding.

3.

You text about the sparrows
that come daily to your balcony feeder,
the stray cat that finds your lap
on a city patio, sleeps there for an hour.

Of this I'm certain:
if a doe crossed your path
she wouldn't be afraid,
would move on her slender legs
into your light.

And I pray to the powers that be:
Let this light prevail.
The world needs kind men.

4.

We agree that it's hard
to collate the days into meaning.

I can't teach you happiness
but I can guess at what it's not.

5.

We exchange quotes.

You send Chomsky:
*The general population doesn't know
what's happening, and doesn't even know
that it doesn't know.*

I send Whitman:
*There will never be any more perfection
than there is now.*

6.

To return is to acknowledge;
to acknowledge is to return.

We talk about death, your father's
the month before you turned thirteen.

Twenty years later you visit his grave.

Healing is a long story
and this one belongs to both of us.

7.

I remind you: each day we must be
lucid with mutiny against despair.

It will change your life,
which dark you choose, which light.

Boots

Calgary: your city,
which today you share with me.

It's late October,
the first fall of the new millennium.

Over perfect martinis we discuss
time as distance, the odd turns
we've clocked and travelled,
the thrill of speed, the metaphor of shoes.

When later we hunt for footwear,
it's with a tacit knowing:
a woman needs to walk, often run.

I find boots the colour of fire
with enduring soles, trust
they will carry me
down the hard roads, the ones
that freeze in winter.

I'll wear them
with the swagger they deserve.

In them I'll cross
into the future, fearless.

Broken

Broken, smaller, less.

The long slide to the depths
where, having fallen silent,
the soul continues despite
careening.

Dust moves, settles;
rust grows.

No redemption
in the ravening night, only
the farthest alone of aloneness.

The love between us
mattered once.

I slip into this confession
as if it were necessary sleep,
comforting and kindred, sink
into muddy knowledge:
fate is the fate
of all relationships.

Moving On

Remarkable, the tributaries of choice,
the offshoots of one decision,
how they continue.

Remarkable too
how different the landscape looks
when the warm light of nostalgia
grows dark.

What I've learned:

> I read maps best
> when you're not with me.

> The journey was never yours
> to give or take.

> Fire has no etiquette,
> burns with impunity.

> There are rocks in all the rivers
> but the water keeps moving.

> I no longer think of you
> as someone I need to forgive.

Indifference

I've heard it said
that the true sign of a truly ended love
is not anger, but indifference.

I consider you, my past loves,
the important ones who once mattered,
the ones with whom
my deepest hurts are buried.

I think of you, but in passing only,
as a passenger notices the shifting landscape
through a car window.

Oh, how I coopered my heart
for each of you, believing you
to be the last one.

Imagine my surprise
when I realize how easy it is
to forget you.

Welcome

The old doubts shoulder in, nudge
the heart's ramparts
with their callous cold noses.

But the heart holds strong,
wants to celebrate
the summer chirring of life,
the frivolous breeze,
the exuberant lie-under sky
in all its blue hyperbole.

It's ready to welcome this love
that comes in holiness and in faith,
this love that breaks it open,
makes it grow.

Return

Where there is renewal
there is redemption.

The tectonic plates
jostle in the depths:
there are seismic changes
in the undercurrents.

In your hands I thaw.

My heart opens, a crater
unfolds at its dark centre,
and heat glows forth
like a buried sun lighting
for the first time.

The past melted us down
but we emerge with wings.

Together we are a flight
and a brightening.

Acknowledgement

To live back and forth like the ocean,
with that much vastness.

When your love washes over me,
I never think of drowning.

What Is True

My love, you know these are true:
the Norway maple canopied
above us, the changing lake
with its steady horizon, the sharp heavy rocks
at the water's edge, the returning cardinals.

True: your hands, in which I am held
and which I hold (such safe fierce pleasure).

Between us a certain beauty
and a small recklessness,
and a gracious trust that doesn't diminish.

Our home is true, and within its walls
what is given and received is true also.

We sit in our newly blue chairs,
drink wine as the sun sets.

We painted them in the basement
as Patsy Cline sang "Crazy"
and the hours passed as hours do.

Now, in this oddly together summer,
we couple ourselves
to hope, its heart-healing sweetness,
and allow ourselves to believe
in what is true.

Centre

Poetry

Tourniquet that keeps the blood in,
torque that drives the flow.

Glorious paradox, still force.

Beauty in Isolation

You fold in and in on
yourself until finally
after the last fold
you are a small
but perfect
origami.

Portrait of the Poet as a Young Girl

1.

She reads biographies late into the night,
dreams herself into a literary future.

What she reads, she can imagine;
what she imagines, she can create.

I celebrate her naïve wisdom,
her calling out to glory, as she fills
the pages with serious joy,
the black ink of *I am*, the human need
to leave a mark, to fill a space.

I watch her journey forward,
one extension of herself after another.

She is unbound and determined.

She will not be cajoled out of poetry.

2.

She uses her poetic licence,
invents words, and words
contain more than themselves.

Imagicate

A new word on a new page.

I magic ate

She adds herself in, thinks magically.

I imagicate

I create magic; therefore I am.

The Story

You wake up knowing
there's a story that has chosen you:
your mouth, your words.

It assigns
and expects you to deliver.

Without you
the story has no voice.

It's a serious business,
taking on the story.

It wants you to witness the rain,
say what you see.

It wants you
to articulate the impossible:
the inflections of shimmering,
the dark universe
before it ignited into stars.

The story's craving is charged
with elsewhere, but rooted
in the now of here.

Such a craving demands love.

This is why
the story has sought you out.

It understands that you've survived
both stasis and transition,
both lightning and the fulgurites
it leaves in the sand.

The story trusts that you will sing it
from the ashes of what birthed it
and let it live.

Incantation

Show me the badlands and the grasslands,
the wet lands and the dry lands,
the sun lands and the snow lands,
the lowlands and the highlands,
the near lands and the far lands,
the lands of plenty, the lands of less.

Let me travel the earth
unfettered by presumption
or excuse-finding prejudice.

Permit me joy in my words
and calm in my ecstatic watching.

And when you pull my soul
from the yearning world,
let my exit be as beautiful
as the whale's breach
or the sun's breaking.

Incidental Contemplations

1.

I am small and immense,
plural.

Like Whitman
I contain multitudes.

You who hold me now
will hold another me
later.

2.

Change:
the beating heart of things.

Think of Pompeii
buried, excavated.

The shards of jugs,
the fine mosaics,
the frescoes of earthly heaven.

Consider:
the small box your grandfather made,
the dance of his dexterous hands
held in the wood.

A lit match could transform this
forever.

3.

And then there are the words.

I too am a guilty trapper
but oh to free them!

To pry open the gates of meaning
and let the wild words run
exultant as horses.

4.

One thing I've learned:
you can't impose your foot
on the river.

5.

I count my ballasts
and my balances,
am found wanting.

It has occurred to me that
I don't do well in captivity.

I'm an escape artist
struggling with the tropes.

Maggot or magus?

Who decides?

6.

In the museum
we forget
that things once ran.

7.

Cavort, caress, don't cower.

Trust the hawk swoop,
the shooting green tendril.

Do the sun work that can be done
only in the light.

Like the relentless windblown waves
keep on cresting, crashing,
coming back for more.

8.

I wish for lucid dreams.

I long to ask the birds
the colour of their waking.

The day is a trickster
and there's so little that I know.

9.

Moment by moment
time captures us.

But truth is not transient
and in these deviant days
what haunts us will survive.

10.

Daily we make
the pilgrimage toward hope
(far away
though often rumoured).

Daily we admire
the crooked spine of love,
how it teeters, tries
to hold us up
in this lonely world.

Then the shock of stars
when the night clears,
and we happen, for a moment,
to look up.

The Heart from Afar

The heart from afar
is a house of longing
or a four-chambered dungeon,
maybe a crib.

Perhaps it's an old boat
rudderless, riddled with rain,
perhaps an empty nest.

From afar
the heart is an elusive city
glittering with promise
or a constellation
in the dark distance.

It's impossible
to truly see the heart
until you're close to it,
and then—
at the very moment
you think you understand,
it vanishes.

That Moment

That moment when you're still
young enough not to care
that you walk alone
in late October's early darkness,
streetlights already on, windows lit,
home beckoning.

That moment, eventually,
when you think
you understand solitude,
its profound and particular hues.

And much later,
that moment when memory
stops you on the road, strikes
with the force of Hopper's *Railroad Sunset*,
its peopleless landscape
(at once sad and exultant)
waiting for a train.

Sometimes It's Hard

Sometimes it's hard
to consider the losses,
the cherished windmills
we tilt toward,
the existential sky
which doesn't care
whether it's blue
or if we're looking.

My heart, shucked
of its complacence,
mourns the endings.

Even the oblivious deer
have their destinies,
the flowers their fates,
and the careless birds
fly off, don't look back.

Knowledge

What the bird knows:
the sky is deathly cold in winter
and flight isn't always upward.

What the tree knows:
each leaf is a life
born of aggressive secret idleness.

What I know:
love is like glass
and every happiness
is difficult in its own way.

Insomnia

That moment—3:00 a.m. in red numbers—
when the muscle metronome—the fast heart
ticking, ticking, ticking—insistent drummer
beating double time in the mind—when you know
it's time, and it hits you over and over
persistent—you're not getting younger—
and then the feeling, that feeling you get
when for sure you know.

Body

I let you down, embarrassed
at every turn by your nakedness.

The body of itself, for itself,
far from the pleasure of others,
the vain discontent of mirrors—
all this I rejected.

I took for granted how you ran me
exuberant through my days.

I lazed on couches, fed you
drink and indifference,
passed on dancing.

I faulted your hips, your thighs,
found you in every way wanting.

Yet still you persevere
and finally, humbled by age,
I let your strength lift me.

She

She is like darkness
but she isn't dark.

She arrives unbidden, stark
and moving, a singer of dreams,
a seer of secrets.

Through her I discover promise
and meaning, the fragility of love.

She is in me and of me,
amusing muse, harbinger of music,
a girl, a woman, a feral crone.

It takes me years to recognize her,
even longer to understand
that she's unfounded and whole,
a sacred ubiquity
that no mirror can reveal,
no death encompass.

The Tigers

In my sleeping night
the tigers groom themselves,
inconsolable.

They know that (teetering
between hope and despair)
even the angels can be savage
and not all truth can be salvaged.

Yet they keep vigil
for the wild that riots,
the soul that roars.

They trust that somewhere
someone dreams
of recreating the world.

You Stand

You stand by the evening window, watch
the lakers on the horizon line, their stacks
lit up like birthday candles.

The lake has lost its daytime striations,
its Rothko rectangles of green and blue.

Along the shoreline the civilized lights
glimmer, a necklace of distant jewels.

Inevitable: each surge of wave recedes
and hard-won courage shrivels in the fallen light.

Every waking leads to sleep
so keep your eyes open while you can.

Without your attention:
nothing but the dissolution of the world.

Transformations

1.

You rise into the summer solstice
with conviction, that foolish sun-aimed arrow.

In the immense arms of love
you become water, become light.

For that moment there's nothing
unflowing in you, or dark.

2.

Your shoulders burst into wings,
your throat fires:
the astonishing moment thrown open.

It's a long process, this appearing.

What will you do with flight and voice,
this perfect pairing?

3.

Sometimes the light hides.

You brandish your small umbrella
in the hard fall rain, know that soon
it will be a storm, a deluge.

You press forward, impervious.

You're a continuous becoming.

You will survive.

A Good Darkness

It's never easy, the patience to see
if happiness will happen.

But sometimes
we remember to breathe,
and humbled
by the cosmos, the sheer reckless
infinity of it, we stumble
into a deep knowing,
the benediction of saviours
(in this case the embracing moon).

Last night
I could not have imagined
this understanding.

Yet tonight, as we sit
by the burning logs, ecstasy
of air and spark surging
toward the black sky,
ancient fire singing back
its holy light to the stars,
gratitude moves through me
quiet and fluid and forever.

Rescue

The lake glimmers its blues,
the trees shimmer.

In the garden: summer's lush bounty,
the vivid joy of greening.

Everything is spirited with light,
willing toward beauty.

If you can find the words,
even the heaviest sadness
will lighten.

The day diminishes
but the sky, festooned with sunset,
continues to celebrate.

When the night comes
bearing stars and moonlight
into the darkest darkness,
I give myself over
to radiance, gift myself hope.

I let poetry save me.

Praise Song

Each day we wake
and there it is, the world,
and we are in it.

This morning after rain
the sky's sleight-of-hand: the way
the light suddens and miracles
everything it touches.

The lake a backdrop for all
that is immediate and tangible:
the cardinal on the feeder, the squirrel
beside the blue pot and its red geraniums.

I bring the first coffee to my lips,
pledge allegiance
to the reckless greens of summer,
the delicate wings of birds.

The world is not new
but we are.

The Aim

To accomplish life in all directions.

To be as music, soul without form.

To mine the exaggerated moods of age,
surface without wanting.

To accept the ongoing departure that never ceases.

To wake each day with an undiluted knowing,
strong as granite, sure as death.

It Is Only

It is only
as the nearness of death
whittles us down to
our ultimate nature, and
with each rising
we startle ourselves into
the sacred light like newborns,
that we dare finally
to recognize the incredible
when it rears its beautiful head,
declares itself.

Fall Artistry

Gone, the summer greens;
don't mourn them.

Admire instead
the trees' bright surrender,
the audacious leaves
flaring and flashing, exuberant
and intemperate,
before finally
they relinquish the branch,
their vital show.

End like the leaves.

Charge your last volley
with a colour-burst.

Detonate your wild
before you go.

Spiral

You continue to spiral
toward an ending
not yours to call.

Everything you love
is what has happened to you.

Everything you fear
is what has happened to you.

All is all there is.

The heart is revealed
deep in the story
that most hides itself,
and what you find at the centre
is never what you expect.

Enough on this day
to be enormously alive.

Notes and Acknowledgements

The title "The Eye Is the First Circle" is from a line by Ralph Waldo Emerson: "The eye is the first circle; the horizon which it forms is the second; and throughout nature this primary figure is repeated without end."

The phrase "wild and precious" in "Sunday Drive, Niagara" refers to Mary Oliver's poem "The Summer Day": "Tell me, what is it you plan to do / with your one wild and precious life?"

The Janis Joplin quote on p. 32 appeared in Michael Lydon, "The Janis Joplin Philosophy: Every Moment She Is What She Feels," *The New York Times Magazine*, February 23, 1969.

"Spring Meditation" was published online as part of the *Creation in Isolation: Why Hope and Beauty Matter* project of Mark Raynes Roberts, spring 2020.

"A 21st Century Poem for Gloria Steinem," "Courage," and "Experienced Music" were published online in *WordCity Literary Journal*, March 2021.

"The New Normal," "Beauty in Isolation," and "A Hellish Season" were published online in *WordCity Literary Journal*, March 2022.

"2020 Vision" and "The Given" were published online in *The Quarantine Review*, Issue 12, July 2022.

"Resistance" was included in *Poets for Ukraine*, a fundraiser anthology compiled by David Brydges, 2022.

"My Mother Annotates a Book of My Poetry" and "Despite Everything" were published online in *WordCity Literary Journal*, September 2022.

"Fall Artistry" accompanied the autumn panel of *Four Seasons: A Collaboration with Nature*, an outdoor art installation by Mark Raynes Roberts at the Jardins de Métis, July 8 to October 2, 2022.

"What Is True" is for Jeanne Hamilton.
"Conversations with My Son" is for Brendan McCarney.
"Courage" and "Another Harvest Moon" are for Darlene Hareguy.
"Boots" is for Aritha van Herk.
"It Is Only" is for Lara Lorge.

Thank you to Carole Giangrande for feedback on ten of the poems included here.

To Patricia Abram: Thank you for the care, insight and understanding with which you read and commented on the *Circle Tour* manuscript.

My heartfelt appreciation, as always, to the Inanna team—especially Brenda Cranney, Val Fullard and Renée Knapp, and also Ashley Rayner—who continue to produce beautiful physical homes for all the words. And a posthumous thank-you to the irreplaceable Luciana Ricciutelli, so loved, so missed.

Finally, to Jeanne Hamilton: You have filled my life with kindness, generosity, joy and so much light. This book is truly for you.

Circle Tour is **Eva Tihanyi**'s ninth poetry collection. She has also published a volume of short stories, *Truth and Other Fictions* (Inanna, 2009). Tihanyi, who taught English at Niagara College from 1989 to 2020, now writes full time. She lives in the Port Dalhousie neighbourhood of St. Catharines, Ontario. For more information, visit www.evatihanyi.com